take the dimness of
my soul away

Praise for *Take the Dimness of My Soul Away*

"Bill Ritter has always been exceedingly insightful and a consummate interpreter of life. His son's death, as he says, dimmed his soul, but with time birthed extraordinary understanding and even gratitude. Reading this tender story, in reality a sermon diary, reawakened my confidence in God's healing gifts." —Donald A. Ott, retired United Methodist Bishop

—◈—

"With the language of a gifted poet, the eye of a portrait artist, and the heart of a faithful pastor and loving parent, Bill Ritter takes us on a poignant God-shaped journey toward healing and wholeness—his and ours. In a world that too often offers superficial answers to poorly-framed questions, Ritter powerfully displays what it means to live with and through the deepest questions of our lives. These sermons are for anyone who has lost a loved one to suicide, or contemplated suicide, or loved someone who has contemplated it. And they are also for anyone who has felt the fractures and fissures of life's brokenness. They are for all of us. Out of Bill and Kris Ritter's personal pain, we are offered a precious gift—healing and life-giving sermons that restore light in our souls." —L. Gregory Jones, Dean of the Divinity School and Professor of Theology, Duke University

take the dimness of
my soul away

healing after a loved one's suicide

william a. ritter

MOREHOUSE PUBLISHING
A Continuum imprint
HARRISBURG • LONDON • NEW YORK

Excerpt used as frontispiece from *The Longing for Home* by Frederick Buechner. Copyright © 1996 by Frederick Buechner. Reprinted by permission of HarperCollins Publishers.

DONE TOO SOON
© 1971 Prophet Music, Inc. All rights administered by Sony/ATV Music Publishing & Music Square West, Nashville, TN 37203. All rights reserved. Used by permission.

Excerpt from a sermon by Mark Trotter used by permission.

Excerpt from a sermon by Rev. James Brown used by permission.

Morehouse Publishing, P.O. Box 1321, Harrisburg, PA 17105

Morehouse Publishing, The Tower Building, 11 York Road, London SE1 7NX

Morehouse Publishing is a Continuum imprint.

Cover art courtesy of Profimedia/Superstock
Cover design by Laurie Westhafer

Library of Congress Cataloging-in-Publication Data

Ritter, William A.
  Take the dimness of my soul away : healing after a loved one's suicide / William A. Ritter.
      p. cm.
  Includes bibliographical references.
  ISBN 0-8192-2104-X
  1. Suicide—Religious aspects—Christianity. 2. Suicide—Sermons. 3. Sermons, American. I. Title.
  HV6545.R57 2004
  248.8'66—dc22

      2004001379

Printed in the United States of America

04 05 06 07 08 09   10 9 8 7 6 5 4 3 2 1

contents

—⚏—

*If preachers are going to talk about hope, let them talk
as honestly as St. Paul did about hopelessness. Let them
acknowledge the darkness and pitiableness of the human
condition, including their own condition, into which
hope brings a glimmer of light.*

*And let them talk with equal honesty about their own
reasons for hoping . . . not just the official, doctrinal,
biblical reasons, but the reasons rooted deep in their own
day-by-day experience. They have hope that God exists
because, from time to time, they have been touched
by God. Let them speak of those times with candor
and contriteness and passion, without which all the
homiletical eloquence and technique in the world are
worth little. Let them speak of those moments, not like
essayists or propagandists, but like human beings speaking their hearts to their dearest friends . . . who, at any
given point, will unerringly know whether they are
speaking truth or only parroting it.*

—Frederick Buechner, *The Longing for Home*

—⚏—

And each one there has one thing shared:
They have sweated beneath the same sun,
Looked up in wonder at the same moon,
And wept when it was all done
For being done too soon.
For being done too soon.

—Neil Diamond, "Done Too Soon"

foreword

The threads that came together to bring this book into being are full of mystery and genuine surprise. In 1985, I felt called to leave the denomination into which I had been born and had served as an ordained minister for thirty-two years and to move into "another Room of God's Great Church," for the rest of my clergy career. I enrolled in the Episcopal Theological Seminary of the Southwest in Austin, Texas, in August of 1985, and became prayer partners with a classmate named Rodney Quainton, who was a former banker from New England and was also beginning his pilgrimage toward the Episcopal Priesthood. A friendship was born between us that has lasted and deepened for over two decades now. Life has carried both of us into many unexpected places, and it was through Father Quainton that I was invited to spend a meaningful weekend leading a Teaching Mission at the First Methodist Church in Birmingham, Michigan, where I met that church's Pastor, Bill Ritter and his wife, Kris. As you will learn from this volume, our lives quickly connected in deep and profound ways.

Something of my own journey through the Valley of the Shadow of Grief over the loss of a child had touched Bill years before, and in our days together, the anguish that lies at the heart of this book came out in honest and heart-rending authenticity.

After this deep and searching encounter, Father Quainton sent me copies of the sermons that describe the journey that Kris and Bill have traveled in the last ten years. It is significant that Dr. Ritter did not mention the possibility of publication of this material. There is a humility in this Methodist minister that is most unusual and admirable indeed. My wife, Ann, and I were both so moved by his life and his words that I took the liberty of submitting these deeply moving sermons to Debra Farrington of Morehouse Publishing. Nothing I have ever done pleases me more.

What you are about to experience is a remarkable blending of mind and heart. Here is a father, husband, minister, friend, and, above all, honest human being, who unabashedly unpacks his heart as to what it was like to love and lose a beloved son in the most tragic of ways. We parents rarely speak openly about it, but we expect our children to bury us, rather than the other way around. All loss or bereavement is horrible, but there is a dimension of pain from the death of a child, especially by suicide, that is unique and severe indeed.

Such is the awesome saga that awaits you in this

slender but powerful life story. Another grieving father told Bill Ritter that he expected to make it through, ". . . because you made it." My prayer is that the publication of this book will have a similar impact on countless other fellow strugglers. Merely to survive such a trauma is one thing. To emerge a decade later as such an articulate gift-giver is something even more amazing. May this story provide you hopeful resources for the living and the writing of your own story.

> John R. Claypool
> Atlanta, Georgia
> February 4, 2004

introduction

Leaving her husband, dying in the dining room, to answer the phone in her kitchen, Shirley returned to announce to me, "It's someone looking for you." This was strange, given that I had told no one of my intent to visit my parishioner and friend, suffering through the final days of Lou Gehrig's disease. But my secretary, guessing where I might have gone, had guessed right.

"There's a policeman here who is waiting to see you," my secretary told me. "I told him I wasn't sure when you'd be back, or if you would be back. But he said he would wait all afternoon if necessary. When I tracked you down at Lee and Shirley's, I asked him if he wanted to talk to you, but he simply asked that I have you come back to your office as quickly as possible." Telling her I would, I did. All the while, I found myself wanting to go anywhere else but there, to see anyone else but him. There was no way his news would be good news. And there was one very possible way his news would be terrible news.

We had worried for weeks about our son, Bill, first-born and oldest by some seven years. Bill had a brilliant mind, but he had recently been troubled of spirit, never more than since his termination from a law firm that previous January. Though he could perform the tasks demanded, he fell short of the speed required, or so they said. As an attorney, argumentation was his long suit. The preparation of briefs, however, was his short one. Then age twenty-seven, Bill had been recently diagnosed with adult attention deficit disorder. That diagnosis answered twenty years' worth of questions for him and for us. Teachers, finding him unfocused, blamed it on the boredom often associated with the gifted and nudged him into accelerated academic programs for others like himself. And while Bill was able to solve complicated problems, debate teachers at the drop of a hat and memorize (photographically, it seemed) entire books of baseball statistics, he read few novels, wrote fewer essays, and learned the art of enrolling in classes where grades would be determined by short-answer testing.

He mastered law school through study groups, and his election to "moot court" reflected an elevated class standing. He prepped for the bar exam using audio-tapes, and an extended internship won him kudos from the seasoned attorneys of a large automotive manufac-turer. But he needed to learn litigation, so he joined a small firm, which promptly dispatched him to the library, where his light did not shine. So mere months after starting, he was finished. First with the firm. Then with his life.

Less than four months after his dismissal, Bill died by his own hand, either very late on a May Monday or very early on a May Tuesday. That's what my secretary had called me back to the office to hear. My office was the senior minister's office at the First United Methodist Church of Birmingham, a large congregation in an affluent Detroit suburb, where I had been appointed to serve eleven months prior. Our move to Birmingham coincided with Bill's move into his own apartment. New job. New digs. New car. New life. Everything seemed to be going his way. And ours. Our younger daughter, Julie, was completing her second year at Duke University. In fact, my wife, Kris, and I planned to leave later that afternoon to retrieve Julie for the summer. The van was packed. The same van I was now driving back to the church, where a pair of stunned secretaries and one stoic police chaplain waited.

Upon entering my office, he suggested I might want to close the door. Whereupon he said, "Mr. Ritter, I am afraid I have some very bad news to share with you. Sometime just before, or right after, midnight, your son completed a successful suicide." Those were his exact words, his only ones. I suppose past experience had taught him to put it straight, keep it short, and wait for it to sink in. There were but three key words in his sentence, all of them starting with the letter *S*. I knew the word "son" meant Bill. And I knew the word "suicide" meant dead. Given my tendency to associate success with achievements of a positive and victorious nature, however, I stumbled over the word "successful." Why would anyone think to link an adjective like "successful" with a noun like "suicide"? Why couldn't Bill have failed?

But failure was not in his plan. He had purchased the gun with foresight, and attended to other details with a thoroughness not commonly associated with his nature. He had gone with friends to Chicago for a wedding (where, according to his buddies, he had been his old self, even to the point of taking the stage at a karaoke bar and singing Frank Sinatra's version of "New York, New York"). Then, on the ride back to Michigan, he told his best friend how lucky he had been to have the parents he had. And with other futures having been looked after, Bill closed out his.

The police chaplain inquired about the where- abouts of my wife. I told him of our plan to meet after work and depart for Duke. He announced his intention to accompany me home and await her arrival. He gave me no choice in the matter. So we went, and we waited, which is as hard, even nine years later, to write about as it is to recall. As a pastor, I have been called upon to deliver the news of a tragedy more often than seems fair. But never to my own family.

What followed is still a blur. Word, having reached the streets, brought a slew of colleagues to the house. Friends appeared shortly after Kris did. And after two hours of being hugged, held, and prayed over, we were on a flight to Durham to tell Julie, bring her back to Michigan, and begin the heart-wrenching task of saying good-bye. Twenty-six hours later, we were back in Detroit, greeted by a house full of family and friends. The following night, there was a reception at the church with a line of well-wishers that completely circled the building. And on Friday afternoon, two thousand mourners filled the sanctuary and overflow spaces for Bill's service. Given the public nature of our lives, it seemed as if everybody knew. And given the personal depth of our relationships, it seemed as if everybody cared, which was, depending on the hour, as overwhelming as it was comforting. It was both the bane and blessing of my profession to go into a super-market and have the cashier say, "You don't know me, but I want you to know how sorry I am about your son."

Expressions of kindness are limited only by the scope of the human imagination. And we had some incredibly imaginative friends. Some wrote letters. Others sent flowers. Many gave dollars. Still others made places for us at their tables. One colleague thought that the gift of a punching bag might be just the trick. It wasn't, but the chuckle it engendered brought its own measure of relief. And then there were the books, sent mostly by clergy. After all, wordsmithing is how we hammer out the rough edges of theology. We were the beneficiaries of countless suicide survival stories, written by people driven by a conviction that there was a calling in their catastrophe and that writing a book was it. I read those books. To be more accurate, I read some, but not all. But never once in those early days did I say, "There's a story in this experience that others need to hear." In those early days, I wasn't able to discern any blessing in Bill's passing. I doubted that his death would make me a better person . . . a better pastor . . . a better preacher . . . even a better friend. So there was no book from my hand. And invitations to keynote seminars on suicide (or resource yet another group of "Compassionate Friends") were sifted carefully and accepted sporadically.

But the Myers-Briggs people, who study personality types, tell me that I am an ENTP, meaning that (among other things) I tend to process feeling through think-ing. In other words, when Kris asks me how I am feel-ing about something, the first words out of my mouth are likely to be "I think . . ." Worse yet, I am never quite sure what I think about something until I attempt to articulate it. So while I know that preaching is more than self-therapy, I find preaching essential to self-discovery. Speaking leads to understanding, and finally to getting in touch with what I really think and feel.

I preached on Bill's death five times. The first sermon was delivered twenty-three days after his memorial service. The fifth was preached nearly nine years later. I didn't deliberately set out to preach any of them. Each was a response to events in my life or nudgings of the Holy Spirit. As to whether there will be more, who can say? I never thought there would be five. But, individually and collectively, they seemed to have been as helpful to others to read as they were necessary for me to write and preach. For years, people have called the church and asked for copies of the "Bill sermons," and we have sent them out.

Crisscrossing the country, they fall into interesting hands and occasion fascinating conversations. This collection is traceable to my Episcopal colleague in ministry, Rev. Rod Quainton, who, as an ecumenical fellow, serves as a member of the clergy staff at First Church, Birmingham. Without my prior knowledge, Rod shared them with John Claypool, whose earlier sermons on the death of his daughter, Laura Lue, prepared the soil for my healing. John, in turn, sent them to Debra Farrington of Morehouse Publishing, and this book is the result. To all these people, I owe a heartfelt thanks. I also want to thank Janet Smylie, who last transcribed them and the congregation of First Church, Birmingham, who first received them. I have been helped out and cheered on by better than I deserve.

Collectively, these sermons will not tell you why somebody you loved left prematurely. Nor will they offer survival techniques preapproved and certified by professionals. These sermons are about the benchmarks on a journey. Mine, certainly. Yours, possibly. We may not be at the same place. But we are covering common ground, which, on good days, might even be deemed "sacred."

Elk Rapids, Michigan
August 2003

when the bough breaks

Bill's memorial service took place on Friday, May 6. On the Sunday following, we breakfasted with out-of-town friends of our daughter's, while the bishop preached at First Church. Seven days after that, Kris and I sat in the pews while the choir sang portions of Brahms's *Requiem*, dedicated to Bill's memory. Leaving church that morning, I felt that preaching couldn't be any harder than sitting, and might even be easier. So on Sunday, May 29, I reentered the pulpit. What I had not taken into account was Memorial Day weekend. As the preacher of the morning, it fell to me to read the roll of the dead. Nothing I said during the sermon proved as difficult as saying my son's name aloud. But painful though it was, and choked though I sounded, it may have been the first moment I knew with certainty that Bill was gone.

—⁓—

Isaiah 40:27–31, Matthew 10:29–31

———

In a week when the Detroit Tigers have lost not one, but two center fielders to disabling injury, I find my thoughts turning to Lucy Van Pelt (of that woebegone "Peanuts" baseball team) who never met a fly ball she could catch or couldn't concoct a good excuse for missing. I'll never forget the day she turned to Charlie Brown and said, "Sorry I missed that fly ball, manager. I thought I had it. But just as I was about to catch it, I suddenly remembered all the others I had missed. I guess you could say that the past got in my eyes."

I know the feeling. Because if anything ails this sermon, it can probably be traced to the fact that I wrote it with whole big pieces of the past in my eyes. For since I last stood in this place to preach on a Sunday morning, my son died . . . too soon at age twenty-seven, and too tragically for reasons that are no longer a mystery to anybody. I still find myself doing all kinds of things and saying, "The last time I did this, Bill was alive. And none of this had happened." But it has happened, and I must find ways to do again what I did before, even though nothing will ever be the way it was before. This is why the past gets in my eyes rather regularly, sometimes in the form of short-term tears, other times in the form of long-term memories, and occasionally in the collage of faces and places that once constituted the world of "the way we were."

How does it feel? It feels bad. It feels sad. It feels empty, achy, and lonely. It feels like everything takes twice as long and means half as much. And above all else, grief feels laboriously like work, except that you don't get any days off . . . perhaps for a very long time. Anna Quindlen, writing in a recent column in the *New York Times*, reflected on the much-too-soon death of her sister-in-law at the age of forty-one, and on a pair of nieces left behind. Concerning her nieces, she wrote:

> My brother and I know too much about their future, since we were both teenagers when our mother died. So if the girls were to ask us, "When does it stop hurting?", we would have to answer in all honest candor: "If it ever does, we'll let you know."

We grieve hardest for what can't be replaced. For in a world where parts are designed to be interchangeable, Kris and I can't go out and get another "Bill." And if we had to lose him this soon, I would have longed for one last good-bye and twenty fewer questions.

So much for how we are "feeling it." I could say

more, and may in time. But grief, as Anna Quindlen also observed, "is one of the few things that has the power to silence us." Which is why everyone who comes near us begins by saying, "We wish we knew what to say." But why should you, when we don't know what to say either?

So "feeling it" will probably have to be done in private. "Facing it," however, is no less important, and is a far more public matter. For we are certainly not facing it alone. To the degree we are standing, it is because we are being pulled up . . . propped up . . . held up . . . and bucked up by an incredible number of kind and caring people, who may not always know what to say, but who are saying it most eloquently. At the close of Bill's memorial service (three weeks ago Friday), our head usher, Carver Wood, was heard to say, "I don't know when I have ever seen such an eloquent testimony to a young man or his family." But when he spoke about "eloquent testimony," he was not just talking about six robed clergy who stood in front of microphones and said something, but about the hundreds upon hundreds of others who sat in pews or folding chairs and said nothing.

I suppose many people came because they felt for us. But I suppose others came because they also felt *with* us. Reading our mail for the past three weeks has convinced us that some of you have also swallowed a pretty deep drink from the river of suffering. One of you sent along a tape of a sermon by Jim Wright (one of my illustrious predecessors in this pulpit). Jim's subject was sorrow. In the sermon, he recounted a legend out of India, wherein a woman who had lost a child came to the Buddha for solace and solutions. The Buddha told her to take a basket and travel from house to house in the village, collecting peppercorns from any family that had not also experienced great loss. Come nightfall, the woman returned, her basket empty.

Albert Schweitzer, that sainted doctor of Lambarene, once wrote about "the fellowship of those who bear the mark of pain." It is a very special fellowship, one that has certainly done its thing for us in spades. Time and again, people have written about things they probably wished they would never have to write about again. But write about them they did. They shared their stories as a way of helping us through our story. A family we have known for thirteen years wrote to tell us about a son we never knew they'd had. Other letters came from parishioners, known less than a year, telling us of children loved and children lost. There were letters that helped us understand Bill, by explaining what depression feels like from the viewpoint of an insider. A twelve-year-old boy who attended Bill's service wrote that he had been recently diagnosed with ADD and placed on Ritalin, yet figured if Bill could have accomplished all the things he did without medication, he would try harder, and with less complaint, to do the same with medication. There was a letter from a girl who, three times, had tried to end her life and pondered her lack of success. There were letters from people who had seen some wonderful things in Bill that were hidden, even from us, and in the telling, gave us pieces of our son to polish and treasure. And then there was the family of the young man whose death, four years ago, occasioned my only previous sermon on suicide. That family not only wrote to, spoke to, and hugged us, but gathered from as far away as Texas to be with us. The "fellowship of those who bear the mark of pain." What a fellowship! What a joy divine!

And some who couldn't place themselves in our shoes projected themselves into our shoes. Some people went home and called their kids. Other people went home and hugged their kids. And a good friend put it all into perspective when he said, "A lot of us are feeling pretty vulnerable. If this could happen to you guys, it could happen to anybody." In a strange way, it was the most affirming thing said about us as a family.

The "whys" abound, of course. But we are slowly coming to terms with the inevitability of mystery. We are not going to get it all figured out. Ever. Which is why there is comfort in George Buttrick's observation that "life is essentially a series of events to be borne and lived through, rather than a series of intellectual riddles to be played with and solved." I guess that in coming to terms with sorrow, courage counts a whole lot more than brilliance.

Perhaps the letter that struck closest to the truth was the one from a couple in California, gone from our lives for twenty years or more, who wrote:

> We have lived in dread, for more than a year, that we would receive a similar call about our daughter. An honors graduate, she has studied abroad not once, but twice. Yet she has reached the point where she can no longer find a reason to get up each day, given that she despairs of ever being able to reach the goals she has set for herself. After our experiences of the last year, I truly believe that some people just do not experience life in the same manner as others do. Their focus does not allow them to see all the good that they bring to the world, but causes them to see only what they have not been able to accomplish.

Feeling it. Facing it. Faithing it. Do believers heal better? Faster? Surer? I think so. But not in an immediately discernible way that diminishes the struggle. There are no shortcuts through the valley, even for those that love the Lord. Still, the One in whom we have believed finds ways to find us—not necessarily because we are looking, but because he is.

Rev. Bob Morley, who flew to Michigan from California to sing one song (even though he came not planning to sing any song), said, "Grace happened to a lot of us in that service, surprising even those who talk about it regularly." And grace keeps on surprising.

Grace came in a magazine editorial recounting Bill Clinton's words at Richard Nixon's funeral. Speaking to a world filled with people who either didn't like Nixon or don't like Clinton, today's leader said of yesterday's, "May the day of judging President Nixon on anything less than his entire life and career come to a close." And I found myself hoping that the same long look of mercy might be granted to Bill as our son and to us as his parents.

Grace also came through a rereading of John Claypool's helpful little book, *Tracks of a Fellow Struggler*, written during and after his ten-year-old daughter's losing battle with leukemia. On the Sunday following her final relapse, after nine deceptively promising months of remission, Claypool preached on that classic text from Isaiah 40, which ends almost doxologically: "But they that wait upon the Lord shall renew their strength. They shall mount up with wings like eagles. They shall run and not be weary. They shall walk and not faint."

Claypool then went on to tell his congregation that, for as many times as he had preached that promise, he was having a hard time believing or feeling that promise. Until, that is, he realized that it was not one promise, but three. And that all three promises need not necessarily be fulfilled simultaneously. This spoke to us in a way that it couldn't possibly have spoken to us fourteen years ago when first we read it. For we are not, now, experiencing all three parts of that promise simultaneously. We are not up there soaring with the eagles, for we lack the wings to fly. And we are not racing down the road like the fast-track kids we once were, defying weariness at every turn, for the Lord has not given us legs on which to run. But as for walking without fainting, that much we have accomplished. We have not yet fallen down. By the grace of God, we are still on our feet, which counts for something. As promises go, one out of three isn't bad. And we'll give God time to make good on the "running" and "soaring" parts.

Finally, grace came through the words of a prominent Presbyterian, James D. Brown, who, when he was the pastor of St. Peter's by the Sea in Rancho Palos Verdes, California, lost his twenty-year-old daughter, Jennifer, to her own hand. From his present home in Louisville, Kentucky, he wrote:

Jennifer committed suicide on January 13, three years ago. I have found myself reflecting on that day ever since, as has my family. It becomes a front-and-center part of your life forever. You find yourself with one foot in this life and one foot in the next. I was working on the yard last fall when we had an unseasonably early snow. We have a beautiful flowering tree in the front yard, and one of the main branches broke off. The leaves were still on the tree but, with the snow on the branch, it was not able to sustain that much weight. So there it was on the ground. And as I was working in the yard, I meditated on that branch and our Jennifer, asking: "Why did Jennifer break so early?"

Later, I came across that passage of scripture in which Jesus says: "Are not two sparrows sold for a penny? Yet not one of them will fall to the ground apart from your Father." Which I think a lot about in terms of Jennifer. Somehow that branch in our yard did not fall outside the providential care of God. And I dare to believe that Jennifer has fallen into the Father's arms.

I have every confidence that such is true. The last sermon Bill heard me preach was on Easter Sunday, when I said every bit as much. Not that I know the particulars of what God has done or will do for Bill. But while I was pondering God's promises, I received a sermon from another California friend named Mark Trotter. In it, he said:

> Every time I talk about the fact that death will not be the end of our journey, someone is bound to ask: "What will it be like?" Just the other day I was visiting the hospital, when a security employee overheard a conversation I was having with a nurse. So he stopped me and said:
>
> "Are you a minister?"
>
> "Yes," I said.
>
> "May I ask you some questions?" he said.
>
> "Certainly," I said.
>
> Whereupon he asked a lot of questions like: "What is it like later? Is there some life after this?"
>
> To which I said: "Yes."

"Well . . . what is it like?" he asked.

"I don't know," I answered, "except that I think it's going to be grand."

To which he said: "No, I mean what will it be like? What's going to happen? How will it look?"

Again I repeated: "I don't know."

So he looked at me and said: "What kind of minister did you say you were?"

Well, I could have pulled out my New Testament, opened it to 1 John, chapter 3, and read: "Beloved, we are God's children now . . . but (as to what comes next) it does not yet appear what we shall be."

Except I do believe this:

For some, it will mean that we no longer have to live under the burden of physical hardship.

For many, it will mean that we no longer have to live with a past that will not go away.

For others, it will mean no longer having to live with a future that will not come.

And for still others, it will mean that some imperfection in our life that continues to cause us to mess up our life, will no longer have the power to hinder us.

My friends, I pray that Mark is right. I pray that God is good. And I pray that Bill is safe. And free. And home at last.

May 29, 1994

an update from the valley

Between the sermon of May 29, 1994, and the one that follows, fourteen months came and went. Kris and I made a pair of conscious decisions concerning our attempt to "deal" (what an interesting verb) with all that was happening in our lives. First, we decided we would not participate in one of the wonderful support groups that others find helpful. Such groups are literally a "godsend" for persons lacking outlets for open sharing and honest conversation. If you live in a world where "nobody wants to talk about it," seeking such folk may be the most important quest of all. But owing to my profession and our personalities, we felt no such deprivation. Everybody wanted to talk about it. So we availed ourselves of support as needed and, to this day, feel comfortable with that decision.

We did, however, keep a regular schedule of appointments with a grief therapist, participating together, knowing that we would seldom be on the same page at the same time and would need someone to remind us of that regularly and interpret that for us creatively. Along the way, we received the bonus of some very practical advice such as designating memorials and surviving holidays.

Still, things were simmering on the back burner of my soul. They only surfaced as a sermon because Bruce Duncan walked into the woods after driving seven hundred miles to be near his parents, only to end his life in a fashion similarly to Bill. Bruce was in his early thirties when it happened. And though he had not been known to Bill, Bruce was well known to us. Ed and Marcia, Bruce's folks, are dear friends. Ed and I both prepped for the ministry at Yale. And not only did Ed officiate at our wedding, but he also preached at Bill's memorial service.

Now it was "return the favor" time. Reluctant to ask, Ed asked anyway. Nervous about saying "yes," I accepted anyway. And after opening the wound partway, I felt sufficiently relieved—and challenged—to open it all the way, which I did on Sunday, August 13. But not without fair warning in a letter to the congregation, herewith reprinted. Of the five sermons, this is the one most focused on suicide, and apparently most helpful to those whose lives have been touched by it.

A YEAR LATER: LETTER TO THE
CONGREGATION

Dear First Church Friends:

Beloved United Methodist scholar, Dr. Albert Outler, left behind an admirable body of scholarly work in the fields of church history and theology. He also left a number of sermons to testify that scholars can speak with deep personal insight and empathy. In one such sermon, he moved from a discussion of the trials and tribulations of greater Dallas to some more personal observations of the neighborhood he knew best.

> Mrs. Outler and I live in a quiet, peaceable neighborhood, and we take long walk-talks in our five-block area almost daily. Over the years we have come to know many of our neighbors. And the better we get to know any one family, the more we learn of the tragic admixture of human happiness and wretchedness in a setting that looks as if it were as favorable an environment as one could find. There is not a single family in our area, as far as we know them, without its share of heartbreak.

Having worked in some extremely "favorable" human environments, I know he is right. I have seen the world's pain behind even the most ornate of doors. And, as a family, we Ritters have had occasion to taste a bit of it ourselves. Most of you know that our first-born son, Bill, Jr., died on May 2, 1994, of his own hand, in response to which I have shared one previous sermon ("When the Bough Breaks," delivered on May 29, 1994). Many of you claim you can see traces of the impact of Bill's death on me elsewhere in my preaching, even though the specifics of Bill's death are not mentioned.

Which is, I suppose, to the good. While each of us retains an essential quotient of privacy, there is no need to hide the things that touch us deeply. Neither, in my case, would such be possible. We are an incredibly public family. Much about our lives reads like an open book. Following last year's Memorial Day sermon, Kris and I drove to our getaway home on Grand Traverse Bay. While motoring north, I realized that the only people "out of the loop" about Bill's death were my Elk Rapids neighbors. Later that same afternoon, I made my rounds, door to door, to the ones I knew best. My neighbor to the south was my first stop. Despite eight years of a shared lot line, I couldn't say I knew him well. Our talk had consisted mostly of shrubs, trees, and lake levels. So you can imagine my surprise in learning that his son had also committed suicide nine years earlier. Deep into our conversation together, I heard myself say, "Tell me when it stops hurting." To which he said, "If it ever does, I'll let you know." He then went on to add that, while everything had changed, some things had healed, and I would grow both through (and from) the experience.

He was right on both counts. The pain has not gone away. But I have grown and learned, although the truths have come hard. For while there is much to learn about grieving from books and pamphlets, none of it speaks exactly to me, or about me specifically. I've had to learn some of the lessons about grieving for myself.

Now it is time to return to the subject in my preaching. Why? First, because I said I would. Second, because some of the benchmarks of my journey have already proven helpful to others. Third, because I am one who doesn't always know what I think until I hear myself say it. St. Augustine once wrote, "I write in order to know what I think." That's probably why painters paint, singers sing, and poets ponder the mysteries of human existence. The upcoming sermon is entitled "An Update from the Valley." The very nature of the title implies that this is only an update, and my process is far from finished. But I have found a secure enough place on which to stand so as to be able to report what—and who—I see.

Sincerely,

William A. Ritter

Deuteronomy 33:26–29, Psalm 23

———

It hardly seems that six days have gone by, given all that has happened since Monday. The place was Elk Rapids. The time was 9:00 in the morning. The day was dressed with sunshine. And I was dressed for golf. Then the call came, telling me that Bruce Duncan committed suicide at the all-too-early age of thirty-one.

Bruce's parents are our friends. Bruce's father, Ed, is my colleague. We went to Yale together. We came to Michigan together. We served over thirty years in Methodist churches together. Ed officiated at our wedding (when our hearts were young and gay) and helped us bury our son (when they were less so). Unlike Bill, Jr., who was our firstborn, Bruce was their last. A studious and sensitive young man, Bruce completed his work at the New Haven Public Library on Friday, withdrew the balance of his bank account in a check made payable to his parents, shared a comfortable evening with friends, and sometime Saturday set out for northern Michigan and the town of Frankfort, to which his parents had retired seven weeks ago. Motoring through Ohio, he stopped and bought a gun. Then he continued until he stopped again, thirty miles from home. After leaving his car by the side of the road, he walked into the woods and didn't come out.

Kris and I visited his family on Monday. I attended to the details of getting pulpit robe and dress clothes from Birmingham to Elk Rapids on Tuesday, and I preached at his funeral in Frankfort on Friday. It was fifty-one weeks to the day since Ed accompanied us to the cemetery in order to inter young Bill's ashes in Kris's family plot. Ed confessed, at the time, that he hoped our roles in this sad and tragic drama would never be reversed. He was wrong. They were.

All last week, people said to us, "Surely this will reopen old wounds." Well, it did—not that the scar tissue covering the "old wounds" was all that thick. But Bruce's death brought it all back . . . from hearing the awful truth to facing an awful death. Already this summer, two other people we know tried suicide and succeeded, while another tried and failed. Interesting, isn't it, that suicide is the one activity where success is failure and failure is success.

But as I said, Bruce's death brought the pain back. Not that it had far to travel. Pat Conroy's long awaited novel, *Beach Music*, begins with a beautiful young wife and mother jumping from a South Carolina bridge. Conroy describes the scene with these lines:

As Shyla steadied herself on the rail, a man approached her from behind . . . a man up from Florida besotted with the intoxicating combination of citrus and Disney . . . and said in a low voice, so as not to frighten the comely stranger on the bridge: "Are you okay, honey?"

She pirouetted and faced him. Then, with tears trailing down her face, she stepped back. And with that step, changed the lives of our family forever.[1]

Is that too dramatic? I don't think so.

I have spent much of my life observing death and dying from a front row seat, one close enough to get my feet, and sometimes my face, wet with the feelings of others. That's because death hurts. All death hurts. Even kindly death . . . friendly death . . . prayed-for death . . . and death that is said to come as a "blessing." It all hurts. So I don't pretend, even for a moment, that what happened to us is necessarily worse than what has happened to you. Such comparisons get us nowhere.

Yet I have learned (from people who know more about these things than I do) that recovery is made

---

1. Pat Conroy, *Beach Music* (New York: Nan A. Talese Publisher, Doubleday, 1995), 4.

measurably more difficult when any one of five factors is present. Those factors are death taking someone young; death taking someone unexpectedly; death taking someone suddenly; death taking someone violently; and death that is self-inflicted.

You do the math. When you add them up, we've had all five.

Still, after Bill's death, Kris and I had to start somewhere. And we did not lack for words of advice, many of which proved to be abundantly helpful. Let me recount three.

First, we were told to actualize Bill's death. Don't dwell on it. But don't dodge it, either. Go back through it. Probe the questions. Sort the papers. Secure the autopsy results. Read the police reports. Talk to Bill's friends. Go through Bill's things. Sift through the final days and hours of Bill's life.

There is no end to the people who will step forward to do that stuff for you. Their aim is to spare you further grief and pain. And it is a good aim, but it is not always on target. Some things you need to do for yourself. And getting in touch with what has happened is one of them.

To be sure, there are limits to how much of this each of us can do at any one time. We all have comfort zones, and I am not suggesting that you violate yours. But there is some value in pushing against them. My friend

Ed went quickly to the site of Bruce's death to see it for himself. Then he went to view Bruce's body. I was advised against viewing Bill's body, so I didn't. Now I wish I had. But how was I to know I would eventually regret not having done so?

Searching through it all, I thought I would find something that would surprise me . . . a clue . . . a conversation . . . a missing puzzle piece . . . a fresh slice of information. But I didn't. From day one, I had a pretty good working knowledge of the factors that contributed to Bill's decision. Yet I kept thinking I would stumble upon something more . . . something that would enable his death to make sense—as I define sense—rather than as Bill defined it in his last days and hours. But the nature of suicide is such that it will never make the kind of sense to me that it somehow made to him. So I keep returning to George Buttrick's line, "Life is essentially a series of events to be borne and lived through, rather than a series of riddles to be played with and solved." What this means is that in coming to terms with sorrow, courage counts for a whole lot more than brilliance.

All we really know is that suicide is usually undertaken as an antidote to pain. My friend Ed said to me, "As much as I hurt for me, I hurt even more for Bruce and what he must have felt." For such pain has a strangely malignant quality, so that even if we could find and isolate the lesion of origin, there is no way to go back and excise it in retrospect. Death's valley casts its shadow, even before death itself does. And it is a darkening shadow. In the powerful words of George Croly's hymn "Spirit of God, Descend upon My Heart," a lament is threaded through the second verse:

> I ask no dream, no prophet ecstasies.
> No sudden rending of the veil of clay.
> No angel visitant, no opening skies,

Which is then followed by the plea:

> Just take the dimness of my soul away.

Translated, that means "I am not asking you to light up my sky, O Lord. Just find some way to keep the 'gray' that is coloring my world from becoming terminal."

But what happens when you open the crayon box and gray is the only color you find? What happens when the best efforts of family and friends can't recolor your world? And what happens when the fire that once warmed your heart grows cold, until the light that once illumined your future goes out? Dimness of soul. That's what happens. And sometimes your soul dims to the point that it costs you your life.

The second piece of advice we were given was "Don't blame yourself." That's so easy to say, but so hard to do. We kept asking ourselves, "What could we have done? What should we have done? What didn't we do?" To which one answer was "You did plenty. And then some. Everybody says so." In point of fact, Bill said so.

Yet guilt is there. That's because it grows, as every parent knows, out of the myth of our own omnipotence. As if we really could make it all go right—or go away—for our children. It starts early in the parenting process, this omnipotence myth. Your child cries out in the night, and even though you can sleep through anything else, you hear that cry. You know that cry. You go to that cry. And whether that cry is occasioned by a nightmare or an ear infection, your response is always the same: You touch your child . . . hold your child . . . cradle your child . . . even as you hear yourself saying, "There, there, it's going to be all right." And you say that, even though you don't know that it's true. You say that, even though there will come a night with a cry you can't answer, a problem you can't fix, a pain you can't remedy. You will not be able to make everything all right throughout your child's lifetime, but you won't be able to shake the feeling that you should. And so forgiveness, when (and if) you finally give it to yourself, is not so much for anything you did or didn't do, but for the fact that at some critical juncture, you were merely human.

The third piece of advice we got sounded paradoxical and required something of a balancing act to achieve. "Keep busy," we were told. "But take time." I chose to overfocus on the first part. I kept busy. I raced back to work. I did a funeral ten days after Bill's, two weddings in two weeks, and a sermon within three weeks of his death. Some of it was clearly avoidance. Not denial. Avoidance. There is a difference. Denial means saying it didn't happen, acting as if it didn't happen, and pretending it didn't happen. Avoidance is when we know full well it happened, but attempt to bracket the pain and put it on the shelf for later.

I feared that if I didn't renormalize things quickly, my life would never be normal. When people told me that it would take years for life to be normal again, they were trying to be kind. But I cringed every time I heard it. The thought that it might take years was frightening and intolerable. I was determined I wasn't even going to give that process months. I would speed the process, even force-feed it, which I did. By sheer heroic effort.

Part of that is simply me. One grieves as one lives,

and I am the kind of person who gets over things by plowing through them. Even though I have never lived on a farm, a plow is an appropriate image: work-related, labor-intensive, and forward-focused. That's me. That's either who I am, or so closely related to my self-perception as to be inseparable from who I am. I once described myself as the Walt Terrell of the ministry. Some of you remember Walt Terrell. He used to pitch for the Tigers. Sparky Anderson liked him. A lot. That was because, Sparky said, "Every fourth day you just hand Walter the baseball and he goes out and throws it. He may not always throw it successfully. He may not always throw it accurately. But when you hand it to him, he never turns it down."

That's how I approached my work, except that my work is not just any work. My work is unique, in that much of it is done for others. I could preach a funeral ten days after Bill died, along with Bruce's funeral on Friday that looked like it could have been Bill's funeral all over again, because there were people who needed what I could do for them more than I needed not to do it. It's Gospel Economics 101. You get back by puttin' out.

Still, there are limits to the "work is therapy" school of grief management, and I reached them. Several people said to me last summer, "After Bill died, we thought you'd take a month off and sit by your lake."

That would have driven me crazy at the time, but it is not without appeal now. One gets tired. If not from work, one gets tired from trying to keep too many feelings on too high a shelf for too long a time. But hold that thought. I'll return to it in a minute.

Before I do, let me append a trio of other words.

About Survival: We are doing it. Surviving, that is. A year, and then some, has passed, but I am smart enough to put no stock in timetables. You shouldn't, either. Still, we feel good about getting this far with our marriage, our health, our jobs, Julie's grades, and our faith intact. Not everybody is so fortunate. When I read about how many others find their losses compounded, I feel good about being where we are. Several weeks ago, a couple came to see me, one week after their son's suicide. They were of a similar age to me, telling a similar story to mine. I didn't know them. I'd never met them. Still, I spent an hour and a half with them. And I hadn't the foggiest idea if I helped them. But I went home and told Kris, "Their words were hard to hear, but good to hear. For while I can remember being where they are, I realized that I am not there now." And that was the first time I gave myself any points for having gained some ground.

Valleys are long and deep and wide. But not every acre of the valley is equally thick or equally dark.

What's more, valleys are bisected by roads. Very few of them are freeways. Only some of them are graded. But they are roads that can be traveled, one way or another.

About Friends: What more can we say? Without friends, we might not make it. It's that basic. I continue to marvel that people who claimed they didn't know what to do or say did both so magnificently. Where did they all come from? Interesting, isn't it, that the phrase "Whatever did we do to deserve this?" can on one day express so much anguish and on the next day so much gratitude. Thank you. Thank you for smiling upon us with the face of Christ more often than I can count.

About Theology: At Bruce's funeral, I said to a room filled with preachers:

> Some will say God had a reason for this. Others will add that God's wisdom is greater than our wisdom . . . that God's thoughts are not our thoughts . . . that God's ways are unsearchable. But I am not one who has ever been content to settle or be satisfied there. Borrowing the well-traveled words of Bill Coffin, I think that when Bruce got out of that car in Mesick, walked into the woods and never came out, God's heart was the first of hundreds to break.

Fortunately, it has always been my conviction that while there may be some pain that God can't explain, there is no pain that God can't embrace.

Which brings me to the loose end I dangled earlier, when I was talking about work and time and the need to feel what must be felt, in the midst of doing what must be done.

Earlier this summer, when I made my first trip to Elk Rapids, I preceded Kris and Julie by a few days. The excuse I gave myself for going early was a backlog of chores that had piled up over the winter. But the real reason I went ahead of Kris and Julie was that I wanted to spend some time by myself. One evening at dusk, I sat on my deck, reading, thinking, looking at the water and letting my mind drift, when suddenly I found myself thinking about little kids. Mine. Yours. Anybody's. And how they like to test themselves by jumping from high places. There they are, standing on the edge of a sofa, straddling a fence post, perched on a stepladder or garage roof, their knees bent and their shoulders hunched. They appear poised and ready to jump. Except they do not jump. Or they don't jump until they first capture your eye (and your ear). "Catch me, daddy," is what they say. "Come over here and catch me when I jump." And you move closer, preparing to do just that. So they jump. And you catch. All things considered, it's a rather remarkable arrangement.

But what if there comes a day when they jump and you can't catch them? Because your arms aren't long enough . . . strong enough . . . quick enough . . . or near enough. When my friend Ed described walking into the woods with his daughter, he said a most interesting thing: "We were able to see where Bruce fell." But the tragedy was that they weren't able to stop Bruce from falling.

I couldn't catch Bill, either. But then again, he didn't tell me he was going to jump. Neither did he wait for me to get my arms in position. Thinking about this on my deck at sunset, I cried and cried. Then I looked down at my book and saw the verse from Deuteronomy —33:27—that had triggered this line of thinking in the first place.

The eternal God is your dwelling place, and underneath are the everlasting arms.

And I realized that though I missed Bill, in that I failed to catch him, and continue to miss Bill, in that I no longer have him, my arms are not the only arms, and my arms are not the final arms. Which means that where he fell is not where he lies.

August 13, 1995

making it

All that really needs to be said about this sermon can be inferred from its title. The phrase "making it" suggests a turn for the better. It hints at recovery. More to the point, it speaks openly about recovery.

Another tragedy involving two young men prompted the creation of this sermon. The boys died as a result of an automobile accident in Arizona, which had the effect of taking a can opener to my heart. But this time it was different, for this time I knew the heart was capable of healing.

In recent years, it has become fashionable for clergy to apply Henri Nouwen's wonderful phrase "wounded healer" to a theology of pastoral presence. This is not only good theology, but good Christology. We who follow Jesus need not hide our hurts. Not all wounds need covering. Even in the pulpit. Especially in the pulpit. People need to know that even preachers have been through some wars and accumulated some scars. But they also need to know where and how healing is taking place. According to 1 Peter, we should always be prepared (one suspects at a moment's notice) to give an account of the hope that is in us. This assumes there is hope in us. And though it took a little over two years to get there, this sermon is that account.

Matthew 5:4, Psalm 91:11–12

———————

Where does a sermon begin? I suppose this one began with a conversation that took place a couple of Sundays ago during our outdoor coffee hour. Rob and Jayne came up to say their good-byes and to express their thanks. Given the events of the last few weeks, most of you know their story. Rob and Jayne used to be neighbors, living across the street from the church. But they did not attend our church in those days. They began attending in earnest only after moving miles away. They never really joined our congregation, but filled a pew on most Sundays over the last couple of years.

Sometime last April, Rob called and invited me to join him and Jayne for lunch. The three of us went to the Ocean Grille. It was the first time I really got to know Rob. And it was the first time I ever met Jayne. They told me that this was going to be one of those "hello and good-bye" luncheons. "We're moving to Arizona," they said. "We're going to start a new life, with new jobs and a new house. But one thing we are going to miss is this church and your sermons." They went on to say some nice things about what I had meant to them and how, without my knowing it, I had helped them. Then we parted company.

I didn't think much about Rob and Jayne until the phone call came from Arizona. I was told a pickup truck had gone out of control, jumped the center lane, and hit one of their cars head-on. Rob and Jayne were not in it, but their sons were. Their seventeen-year-old, Chip, was killed instantly. Their nine-year-old, Chris, was removed from life support two days later. There was a small service in Arizona. But the primary memorial took place in our sanctuary, three weeks ago Saturday. Seven hundred people shoehorned their way into every nook and cranny of this building. I only remember one such service being any larger. But I wasn't preaching that one.

On the following Sunday, Rob and Jayne (along with their daughter, Kate) joined us for worship. They returned one week later to say their final farewells. Out on the lawn, Rob wrapped me up in one of his bear hugs. Then he said, "Come and see us. Call us. Think about us. Pray for us. But don't worry about us. We are going to make it. And the reason we are going to make it is because you made it."

That statement humbled me when I heard it. I didn't know quite what to do with it. We clergy are aware that we serve as models and mentors. Sometimes we'd like to forget that. Sometimes we wish it were otherwise. Sometimes it makes us uncomfortable. But people do watch us. To some degree, people even take their cues from us. They watch it all. Not just our behavior. Not just our character. But the way we carry the faith, and the way our faith carries us.

To be sure, people keep their eyes on the surface stuff . . . the outer stuff . . . the visible stuff. They watch what we say and think and eat and drink. They take note of whether we spit and cuss and fume and fuss. You'd be surprised how many people notice when I buy a new tie. But people also watch the inner stuff. They watch to see if the faith we proclaim is doing for us what we say it will do for others. They watch to see if, as a result of what we preach, there is any joy in our eyes, peace in our hearts, courage in our guts, or strength in our steps. They watch to see if we are people who know the Lord—who know that we are known by the Lord—and who know we share a common bond with others in the Lord, including the obnoxious, obstreperous, and oppositional ones.

Someone once told me, "Never trust a skinny cook." So I suppose you shouldn't trust a thin-in-the-faith preacher, either. Even though this preacher would rather be watched over than watched, I realize I probably can't have one without the other. So I was all right when Rob grabbed me in his arms and said, "We're gonna be all right because you're all right." He'd been watching me, you see. That humbles me, and scares me, too. But it also cheers me, given his claim to have seen something in me that both speaks to him and encourages him to keep going. Maybe that's where this sermon began.

Or maybe it began last Mother's Day. It was a glorious day at Wallace Wade Stadium of Duke University. For it was graduation day . . . Julie's day . . . Mom and Dad's day . . . Grandma and Grandpa's day. The sun was shining down on us, and the Son was welling up in us. We were filled with all the usual feelings—pride, joy, relief, and happiness. And we were filled with gratitude. Especially gratitude. For as we sat in those bleachers, there was the memory of another trip to Durham that very same week two years earlier. It was the trip we took to tell Julie that her brother was dead. Suddenly. Unexpectedly. Prematurely. Violently. And by his own hand. Now here we were, two years later, our family intact. Our marriage, our health, our careers, Julie's degree program and academic standing were also intact. I guess those are signs of "making it." I think it was Kris who first pointed it out to me. But when she said it (and I heard it), both of us smiled.

Or maybe this sermon began when Bill died. And we all cried. Before going to work. I am talking about grief work. Hard, long, tedious, and tiring grief work. With lots of overtime and no days off. And wages that seemed paltry, but eventually began to pay dividends, just as people said such work would, if we kept at it, without skirting or shirking it. Now we even have an occasional day when we don't think of Bill. Or when we do, we are able to remember and miss him without being overwhelmed by the pain.

Grief work was hard for me to do during the first year, so I didn't always do it. I did other work—church work, God's work, our work. All of it was good work, and well-rewarded work. But sometimes it was substitute work for the work I needed to be doing the most.

The second year of grieving began with Bruce Duncan's suicide. I preached his service, and there was something about facing Bruce's death—and seeing Bruce's family—that got to me, leaving me more vulnerable than I had been before. That made the second year harder, longer, and more difficult than the first. People often say that about the second year. Men, especially, say that about the second year. And there was no period any worse than the months when winter came, stayed, and would not quit. How does the hymn put it?

Melt the clouds of sin and sadness,

Drive the dark of doubt away.

Giver of immortal gladness,

Fill us with the light of day.

Henry Van Dyke wrote it. Ludwig van Beethoven harmonized it. And I prayed it. For there was much in me that needed "melting," needed "gladness," and needed to see the "light of day." My problem was not with the earlier work of grief. Anger, I'd looked at. Guilt, I'd looked at. Loss, that too. Those things were far from over. But those things were far from new. My more pressing problem had less to do with overcoming sadness than with allowing myself to embrace happiness. My spirit had moved from terrible to tolerable, and from tolerable to manageable. But I couldn't seem to make the move from manageable to enjoyable.

I recall a conversation that took place two weeks after Bill's death. A man made an appointment, came into my office, and said that he figured we were "soul mates." He, too, had a son who had died under similar circumstances. He told me his story. I don't recall that he really asked that much about mine. Then he said, "I'm doing all right. And you will, too. But the best part of every day comes at the end of the day. That's when I realize I've got one less day of living, leaving me one day closer to dying and being with my son."

He thought I would find that lovely, but I found it frightening. I thought to myself, "I don't feel that way. I don't ever want to feel that way. Because feeling that way will not only wither the bloom from life's lily, but will steal, from my eyes, the ability to see whatever future lilies there might be." Then winter came. And I realized that not only was I missing the lilies, I wasn't really taking time to "consider them" in the biblical sense. That two-year-old conversation came back to mind, leading me to reaffirm, "I don't want to end up thinking what he thinks or feeling what he feels, thereby missing what he is missing in the process." I would hate to think that the best part of any day, let alone every day, would be the realization that I am one day closer to dying.

All of this leads me to the first in a trio of truths I want to share with you. The best way to honor the dead is to love the living. I have been saying that in my funeral prayers for at least twenty years, possibly longer. But I am dense. Sometimes it takes me longer than the average listener to hear what comes out of my own mouth. Which means that while I say it, I don't always hear it. I know that grief is one way to hold people close. But it is not the only way to hold them close. And it may not be the best way to do that. To whatever degree the dead may be aware of what they have left behind them, I doubt they feel honored by our inability to get beyond them. For if our lives stop when their life stops, death has killed twice.

Several times over the last few years, I have buried the husband or wife of a highly successful marriage. In conversations surrounding the funeral, friends of the couple have confided their expectation that the surviving spouse would likely be "gone" in a matter of months. Sometimes I concur with their assessment. But that often makes me a little sad, even though I've never said so, at least not until now.

Instead, I think we honor the dead by turning toward the living, and toward life itself. I'll never forget the widow who, on the morning of her wedding to a widower she met in a grief recovery group, told me, "I think John (my first husband) would both understand and approve of my marriage to Roger. In fact, I think he's probably smiling in heaven right now. John once told me that if he should die first, he wanted me to marry again, if only to show people that what we had was so good for so long, that the thought of being without it would be neither a pleasant prospect for me nor a fitting way to honor him." And when Roger (her second husband) died, she told me, "I thank God for the privilege of having been loved by two of the most wonderful men to ever walk the face of the earth." For, you see, the second husband followed the first in her heart, but never replaced him.

Let me speak personally once again. There is hardly a day that goes by when I don't hear, see, read, or experience something that leads me to say, "Wouldn't Bill have liked this . . . loved this . . . gotten a kick out of this?" It makes me sad and sometimes brings a tear to my eye. But it doesn't mean I should love such things less. What it means is that I should love such things even more.

All of which leads to a second truth, which has greatly enhanced the prospect of my "making it." Namely, it doesn't help the recovery process to think like a victim. Bill's death happened in my life, but it did not happen *to* my life. It was not done to me by Bill, by God, or by anybody else. Bill did not die to make me miserable. He did not die to make his mother or sister miserable. He did not die to make his friends miserable. He died because, at that point of his life, he was miserable—in ways we couldn't fully fathom or successfully penetrate.

I know that a death like Bill's feels like rejection. And I know it is hard to take rejection any way but personally. But I have reason to believe he did not mean it that way, and that he would be chagrined to think I was taking it that way. Several years ago, a preacher wrote:

I do not believe that people who kill themselves are (at that precise moment) capable of understanding and appreciating the pain they are inflicting upon those they are leaving behind. I think their despair is too great for them to see that. I think they may believe they are solving one problem, with scant recognition of other problems they may be setting in motion. Their choice is just that—their choice. Private. Personal. And largely incapable of taking into account the wider impact it will have.

I do, however, have one suggestion for the survivors. Sooner or later, you will need to forgive what you can't understand. For you may never figure it out. And even if you do, the conclusions you reach in your head may not necessarily heal what you feel in your heart. The only way out of your pain may be to start splashing forgiveness in every direction . . . forgiving the one who took the life . . . forgiving yourself for anything you did or didn't do, just before it happened . . . forgiving God for allowing it, or not stopping it . . . and even forgiving circumstances for being so damn hard and weighted against you.

That sermon was preached six years ago. I know, because I am the one who preached it.

Now, having introduced God into the mix via my last paragraph, it is time to voice my third truth. Namely, the same arms that catch the dying also carry the living. The last time I preached upon these matters was fifty-four weeks ago. At the end of the sermon, I quoted those wonderful words from Deuteronomy: "The eternal God is your dwelling place, and underneath are the everlasting arms" (Deut 33:27a RSV). This means that whenever, wherever, and however we fall, God is the center fielder of last resort, the ultimate Catcher in the Rye against whose name no errors have ever been recorded. Nothing escapes God's gaze. Nothing eludes God's grasp. This takes care of the dying. But what of the living? Permit me a closing observation.

More times than I can count over the course of my ministry, I have run into a little piece of prose entitled "Footprints." I have seen it on postcards, greeting cards, and bookmarks. I have seen it framed on walls, mounted on desks, and magnetized to refrigerators. The gist of it is simple. Someone dies and is permitted to glimpse (from the vantage point of heaven) the journey of his or her lifetime. That journey is depicted as a trail of footprints on a sandy beach. There are two pairs of footprints when times were good. There is one pair of footprints when times were less good. "Explain this," says heaven's new arrival. "Who belongs to each pair of footprints?" "That's easy," says the Lord. "One pair is yours. One pair is mine. Step for step. Side by side."

"I see," says the questioner. "But why is there just one pair in the rough times? Why, when I needed you most, did you abandon me?"

The Lord, looking at the same single pair of footprints, answers, "Abandon you? I didn't abandon you. That's when I carried you."

And for years, I pondered that and thought to myself, "That's nice. But why are so many people so taken with it? After all, it's not complex theology or great prose. It's a bit syrupy. A tad simplistic."

That's when I realized that people like that piece of prose, not as a promise of what the Lord might do, but as a reminder of what the Lord has already done. For a lot of people can name a day when they could do no more, climb no higher, walk no further, when the thing that once made them say, "If that ever happened to me, I'd die," happened—and they didn't die.

How did they get through? They don't know. What's more, they can't tell you. But they did. Get through, that is. And to this day, they can't explain it.

So what do they do? They buy a little 79-cent litho, put it in a $50 frame, and hang it on a $100,000 wall. It's about some footprints in the sand and a conversation on the balcony of heaven.

Which is probably as good a way as any to say, "Look, I don't know how it happened. But I once was there. I now am here. And it occurs to me that I couldn't have gotten from there to here all by myself."

August 25, 1996

a taste of honey

As was the case with the previous two sermons, this one was also preached in August, which was not entirely accidental. I tend to lay down some of the workload in August, the better to recharge, some of which happens at our getaway home on Grand Traverse Bay. It is always lovely there, but never more so than in August. The combination of water and deck chairs drives me not only into the pages of a book, but on many days, into the crevices of the soul.

In the sermons thus far, certain authors have surfaced. Names like Buttrick, Buechner, Claypool, and Conroy. Not to ignore the lingering shadow of William Sloane Coffin's wonderful sermon, "Alex's Death," which describes the night his son took an icy curve at an elevated speed and ended up on the bottom of Boston Harbor. But no book triggered the first three sermons. Tragedy triggered those sermons . . . tragedies involving young men with names like Bill, Bruce, Chip, and Chris.

Finally, I offer a sermon without a tragedy for a catalyst. This time, the catalyst was a book of sermons.

The author was my United Methodist colleague J. Ellsworth Kalas. Entitled *Old Testament Stories from the Backside*, it reveals Kalas's wonderful gift for story spinning, so that old, familiar texts suddenly came at you from an altogether different direction.

Because Bill's death does not merit mention until the sermon is 70 percent complete, one might question its inclusion in this collection. But it is about Bill's death from beginning to end, even though (in the spirit of my colleague) I take a long and circuitous route to get there. Once again, recovery is the theme, including a begrudging acknowledgment that I might have learned something I never would have known, while developing a gift I might never have had, were it not for the worst thing that ever could have happened.

Judges 14:1–14

When our daughter, Julie, was very young, we never went anywhere without taking along a bag of her favorite books. We read them aloud to her, over and over again. Most of them we memorized, as did she. But she never tired of hearing them, even though we tired of reading them. And woe be unto the reader who skipped a page, the better to cover the material quickly. The penalty for that breach of literary etiquette was the requirement to go back to the beginning and start over.

We read it all. We read the Dr. Seuss stuff. We read the Richard Scarry stuff. But never did we skip a bedtime without reading *Mickey Mouse's Joke Book*. As to why that topped the list, I didn't know then, and don't know now. But when I stopped in the middle of this paragraph to call Julie to ask if she remembered it, she not only remembered it, but also told me where (in the basement) I could find it.

The humor is basic stuff with a heavy dependence on riddles. Her favorite page featured Goofy rushing to his new job at the Eagle Laundry, leading Mickey to ask him what he did there. The answer: "Wash eagles, of course." And the accompanying picture depicted several bald eagles, still dripping with water and suds, fastened to a clothesline with big wooden clothespins. Of course, to appreciate the humor, a kid would have to be familiar with a clothesline and wooden clothespins. Many children today have never seen a clothesline, now that we have electric dryers.

All of us cut our teeth on riddles. And some of us still sharpen our teeth on riddles. Every culture has them. Even preliterary people enjoyed them. Some riddles take new forms in changing times. When I was a child, we asked, "What's black and white and red (read) all over?" The answer: "A newspaper." In the seventies, however, when the mood of the young turned cynical and the humor macabre, we asked, "What's black and white and red all over?" And the answer came back: "A nun in a blender." Indeed, there are Ph.D. dissertations that undertake, as their sole purpose, the analysis of a nation's humor as the barometer of a nation's mood.

Many years ago, a young man constructed a riddle to mystify his contemporaries. And it is his riddle that both highlights today's text and occasions today's sermon. The young man is Samson, of Samson and Delilah fame. But Delilah is not yet on the scene and in no way figures in the story. This is the period of the judges, along about 1150 B.C., when Israel was ruled, somewhat loosely, by a number of regional chieftains.

For those wishing to place things in proper context, this period comes after Moses, but before David. Samson was one of these judges.

Samson was not the brightest guy to ever come down the pike, and we tend to remember him for his legendary strength. It was said that with nothing more than the jawbone of an ass, he could rout whole armies. And while that may have been stretching things a bit, we get the picture. That strength comes into play in this morning's story, as do two other things for which Samson was known: his roving eye and his less-than-prudent assessment of women.

While wandering in the village of Timnah, Samson notices a certain young woman who pleases him, so he returns home and says to his mother and father, "She's the one for me. I want her. Go get her." It was the duty of the parents, you see, to provide wives for their sons (and, presumably, husbands for their daughters).

Samson's parents are less than happy with his choice, given that this girl has a pair of strikes against her. She is not from Samson's village. And she is not from Samson's people. Samson is a Jew. She is a Philistine. In other words, she is "one of them," not "one of us." So his father says, "Can't you find anybody local?" To which he replies, "I want what I want. Go do your fatherly thing."

So in the company of his parents, Samson heads for

Timnah, where he encounters a young lion ("young" as in athletic, not "young" as in baby). But with his phenomenal strength, coupled with the Spirit of the Lord, Samson tears the lion apart bare-handed, as one might tear apart a kid ("kid" as in baby goat, not "kid" as in second-grade child). That feat impresses me to no end. My grandmother used to kill chickens for Sunday dinner, but never a lion. I have never known anybody who killed a lion. Even my "tough as nails" Aunt Emma never killed a lion, although she could have.

Killing a lion was an important mythic act. Hercules killed one bare-handed, as did Polydamas in imitation of Hercules. And in 1 Samuel 17:36, the youthful David tells Saul that he can go one-on-one with Goliath because, on previous occasions, he has already killed lions and bears. But then, so have the Packers. In 2 Samuel 23:20, one of David's men, Benaiah by name, killed a lion in a pit in the snow. Suffice it to say, lion killing is an act that is as mythic as it is expedient. Anybody who's anybody has done it. Some more than once.

At any rate, Samson kills the lion, leaves the lion, and sometime later, while traveling down the same road, stumbles upon the lion's carcass. But now he finds that a swarm of bees has taken up residence there. For in barren areas, where hollow trees are not available in abundance, wild bees often establish colonies in animal carcasses. Apparently, a dried-out hide provides a perfect home for the bees.

So with the lion's carcass now rich in honey, Samson scoops out a handful and goes merrily on his way. The story gives no clue as to how he fights off the bees. But as readers, we can't have everything. Later, he shares some of the honey with his parents, who enjoy it every bit as much as he does. But he doesn't reveal its origin, given that their tastes may be a bit more squeamish than his.

Cut now to the wedding. Apparently, somebody (presumably Samson's father) is successful in convincing this sweet, young Philistine from Timnah to be Samson's bride. So there is a celebration, a party—a "drinking bout," if you want to translate the Hebrew precisely. We're talking about a seven-day cocktail party, with the actual wedding ceremony taking place at the close of the seventh day. That way, even if someone canceled the nuptials, you still would have had a good reception. In those days, one of the amusements in the course of a wedding feast featured the groom testing his fellows with a riddle, which customarily included a wager or two. In this case, the wager involved some very expensive clothing (Armani suits . . . Ellen Tracy dresses . . . that sort of stuff).

And this is the riddle that Samson presents:

Out of the eater came something to eat.

Out of the strong came something sweet.

What is it?

The answer, of course, is "honey in the lion." Except that nobody gets the riddle. At least, nobody gets it until the bride reveals it. But that's another story, and not necessarily a pretty one, given that it kills the wedding, along with thirty of the wedding guests. So let's not go there. Let's stick with the riddle. Or, to be more precise, let's stick with its answer: "honey in the lion."

Samson was able to find nourishment for living (i.e., honey) in something that threatened to take life from him (i.e., the lion). The lion was, by nature, an eater. But out of his carcass came something to eat. Or, to put it another way, Samson returned to find "a certain sweetness" in the midst of something that could very well have been his destruction.

"Blessed are they," says biblical scholar Ellsworth Kalas, "who learn that there is honey in the lion." But this is sometimes hard to find, although lions are easy to find, in part because lions tend to find us. For by now, you have figured out that I am not talking about four-legged lions, complete with manes and tails. I am talking about other kinds of lions, equally fierce and more than capable, in their own way, of eating us alive or maiming us for life.

Life is full of jungles, which can be anywhere, can't they? And life is also full of predators, who can be anybody, can't they? Sometimes the "devouring" is an inside job, as in the question "What's eating you, my friend?" Having lived in city and suburb, I have seen people eaten in both places. Having worked among poor and rich, I have seen people eaten in both circumstances. Whether it be war and violence, depression and disillusionment, poverty and peer envy, or sickness and bereavement, no one walks the road of life without encountering some hungry lions.

And these lions will pounce. And maim. And cripple. For that is the nature of lions. That is what lions do. If they don't take your life, they will take their toll. Do not, even for a minute, make light of that. For after meeting a lion, you will never be the same. Some people go through a crisis and say, "I've got to get back to my old self." But that's a fruitless quest. You will never get back to your "old self." For the crisis has taken your "old self" with it. You'll never get it back. Ever.

But that doesn't mean you can't come out with something. For one of the strangest, yet most sublime, facts of human existence is that something beneficial can often be harvested from life's most devastating experiences.

When previously divorced people come to me to be

married, I do not turn my back on them because of past failures. Some denominations would make me do so. And a literal interpretation of at least one passage in the Bible would have me do so. But I do not turn them away. Instead, I ask them what they learned about themselves while they were going through their divorce. And I listen carefully to their answer. For I have little interest in what the other person did compared with what they, themselves, discovered. That's because lessons learned, if internalized, may turn out to be "honey in the lion."

History, too, offers us story after story in illustration of my point, people who found something to eat in the thing that was eating them. And I could sprinkle our final few minutes with several such accounts. But unless you have survived the lion yourself, to the point of finding a subsequent cache of honey, or unless you can remember some stunning setback that looked like the defeat of all your dreams, but eventually led to a moment of turning or triumph you'll probably just write me off and go on feeling bitter rather than better, and victim rather than victor.

But I've got to believe that many of you have made a return trip down the old road where the lion lay, and may still lie, and have taken your fistful of honey from his gut, however many years may have passed in the meantime. The key is that you went back down that road. Then you looked for the honey. And upon find-ing it, you reached for the honey, because neither God nor anyone else handed it to you, free for the asking.

Let me be personal. From time to time, I share an updating word relative to the fiercest lion I ever met— or ever hope to meet—in my earthly life. I am talking about the suicide of my son, Bill, some fifty-two months ago. There were times when I felt that lion might very well destroy me, too. In the wake of Bill's death, I lost my "old self" and have never gotten it back. Nor do I expect to.

Shortly after he died, Kris and I made an appoint-ment to see someone Bill had seen relative to his med-ication. And I would be less than honest if I told you that our meeting went well. It didn't. We didn't connect on any level, and no comfort was taken, quite apart from the question of whether any comfort was given.

But Bill's doctor said something I have never forgotten, partly because it made me incredibly angry at the time. She said, "You probably can't see this now, and therefore can't believe it now, but there will come a day when you will actually view Bill's death as a gift."

I suspect she was making reference to things I might learn personally, that I would eventually put into practice professionally. But I didn't want to hear that then. I didn't need to hear that then. And I didn't like being told that then. For I was not ready to have a philosophic discussion about the pastoral benefits of my loss. I was still in what writer Peter Gomes called my "baying at the moon" stage. I was bleeding. And I was looking for someone to do mop-up duty, not perform needle-and-thread stitchery.

Besides, her word "gift" was—and still is—much too strong. Bill's death didn't feel like a "present" then. And it doesn't feel like a "present" now. But she was not entirely off track. For there have been enough tastes of honey in that lion, so as to make life's bread edible—not so much my own bread, but other people's bread.

Since that day, I have buried eight suicides. I have lectured twice on suicide. I have preached three times on my own experience with suicide. And I will do a November workshop for professional grief therapists who deal with suicide as a part of their daily fare. I do not seek such opportunities. But neither do I turn them down. Every time I do one, it is like taking a can opener to my heart. But each time that wound is opened, something of a cleansing takes place. So whether I am doing any earthly good for anybody else, I suppose—in some self-centered way—I am doing something good for me.

But here and there, it does appear that I am doing a bit of good for somebody else, including a lot of people I have never seen. Someone reads one of my sermons and sends me a note. Someone else hears one of my tapes and passes it to a friend who needs it more than they do. And then there's this.

In late September, Kris and I are going to Scotland for a few days. On one of those days, I am scheduled to play golf and have dinner with a friend of a friend, an old Scot named Alistair. Alistair is a retired doctor, recently widowed, and a man of keen intellect and deep compassion, but possessed of little if any religious faith. In fact, when he heard I was coming and that we would be golfing and dining together, he wrote my friend and said, "I'd love to meet Bill and his wife, but does he know I am an atheist?"

My friend wrote him back, telling him that I knew and that I would be "okay with it." But just to give him a feel for me, my friend sent Alistair a couple of my sermons—two of the "Bill sermons." My friend received the following note in response:

Dear Brent,

Thank you for your letter of 4th April. I am really ashamed of this very late acknowledgment. My only excuse is apathy and lack of concentration. However, I am beginning to feel better, both physically and mentally, with the realization that age is catching up with me fast.

I wasn't aware of conveying my misery in my last letter. Thank you for your insight and understanding. And thank you for sending me Bill Ritter's sermons and thoughts following the death of Bill Jr. I can only describe both as brilliant, deeply touching, and must confess to shedding some tears. I have read and reread them many times and shall continue to do so. I have also shared most of his all-embracing thoughts. Never could I have clarified, or rather sorted out, so many thoughts and conflicts so adroitly. And this has helped me to see things more in perspective.

I look forward to meeting Bill and Kris.

I look forward to meeting him, too. I will enjoy the golf. And I will enjoy the meal that follows. I suspect that dinner will be on him, given his claim that he has already found food in my words. What kind of food? Darned if I know. But reading between his lines . . . or lions . . . I suppose it could be honey.

August 23, 1998

a reason to live

Following "A Taste of Honey," I thought I had said enough about Bill's death and had little else to add on the subject of suicide. I knew I would reference it again. I just wouldn't dwell on it. Time had moved on. Life had moved on. I had moved on. Besides, four sermons seemed sufficient to send upon request. Why overwhelm people?

Except for one thing. I had never treated the subject of suicide considered apart from the subject of suicide completed. Yet the issue surfaced from time to time. Frankly speaking, what does one say to someone teetering on the edge? It is one thing to rationalize that those who voice it don't usually do it. Statistically speaking, this may be true. But I realized that some of my reluctance had to do with the fact that I could not talk Bill out of his self-destructive act. Did I believe it could happen? Yes, I believed it could happen. Had I voiced my concern to Bill? Yes, I had voiced my concern to Bill. Had Kris and I taken steps, enlisted allies, and widened the circle of concern to keep it from happening? Yes, we had done all of the above and more. We thought Bill's assurances that he would hang in there and see this thing through were trustworthy. But we were wrong. Along with others. For none of us accurately judged the depth of his pain.

Then I saw the film *The Hours* and agreed to review it for a church-related seminar entitled "Jesus @ the Oscars." Staying alive is one of the film's major themes. Failure to do so—and the ripples such failures create— is yet another. This meant that at least one more sermon begged to be written. Hopefully as a warning. Perhaps as penance.

Psalm 30:4–5, Matthew 16:24–25

Let me introduce you to Bill Muehl, Grosse Pointer by origination, Episcopalian by confirmation, University of Michigan–trained lawyer by vocation, who was rerouted by God in 1944 to New Haven, Connecticut, where he ended up teaching forty years' worth of young mumblers at Yale Divinity School how to preach. Including me.

One of Bill's most legendary stories concerns a cocktail party where he was approached by a man who had had more than a little to drink and was feeling neither pain nor trepidation. Buttonholing my beloved professor, the inebriant said:

Muehl, if I believed all that Christianity bunk, do you know what I'd do? As soon as my children were born, I'd have them baptized. And then I'd cut their throats from ear to ear so they'd go straight to heaven. Why should any man who loves his kids let them go through the heartache of life and run the risk of hell, if he can send them to glory with a single sweep of the knife?[2]

And though it is not generally advisable to talk theology with people who are "three sheets to the wind," I think every seminarian should be required to write a one-page response to that man before being allowed to graduate and go anywhere near a pulpit. Simply put, the question translates, "If eternal life is likely to be so much better than present life, why put up, any longer than absolutely necessary, with a life that cannot help but be measurably worse?" Or if you don't like that translation, let the question read, "When the going gets tough, why don't the tough get going . . . as in, right on out of here . . . beyond this life . . . above this life . . . quitting this veil of tears for whatever follows this life?"

There are multiple answers. But most of them fall under one of two banners. The first banner reads, "Look again, this isn't really a veil of tears. And if it seems that way today, it won't seem that way tomorrow." That's the "things will get better, so don't get bitter" banner, initially hoisted by the psalmist who wrote, "Weeping lingers for but a night, but joy comes

2. William Muehl, *All the Damned Angels* (Philadelphia: Pilgrim Press 1972), 108.

in the morning" (Ps 30:5). Or perhaps it is the answer of Robert Schuller, who tells us, "Tough times don't last, but tough people do." And it is clearly the suggestion of Little Orphan Annie, who, somewhere tonight, will step center stage and sing, "The sun'll come out tomorrow . . . bet your bottom dollar that tomorrow there'll be sun."

Those are all wonderful answers, which will assuredly work. At least they will work until too much time passes and there is no joy in the morning . . . no sun on the morrow . . . no respite from life's tough times . . . or no lifting of life's tearful veil.

Then a second set of answers kicks in. They are collected under a second banner, the one that reads, "All of this is good for you." After all, said C. S. Lewis, suffering is the anvil on which a Christian's character is hammered and forged. Although it must be noted that this was the early C. S. Lewis of *The Problem of Pain*, rather than the late C. S. Lewis of *A Grief Observed*. The early Lewis had much in common with the late Paul, who advised the Romans that "we boast in our sufferings, knowing that suffering produces endurance, endurance produces character, character produces hope, and hope does not disappoint" (Rom 5:1–5). The bottom line of this argument suggests that the hard life prepares one for the good life, and may even be the good life. In fact, suffering might well be described as chemotherapy for the soul, meaning that if it doesn't kill you, it might just save you. There's truth in those answers, too. And they'll work—until the same anvil that forges your character tips over and flattens your courage.

Sooner or later, people come to breaking points beyond which they can no longer go. Nor do some wish to go further. At that time, death's face—to whatever degree death can be described as having a face—strikes a pose that is more friendly than frightening. When that happens late in life, at a point that feels like the "terminus," we call death's friendly face "a blessing" and offer little resistance to it. In the last six months, I have heard all of the following: "I want to go home." "I just want to die and be with Jesus." "Reverend, I'll tell you why I'm not afraid to die. I know I have more people in heaven to say hello to than I have here to say good-bye to." And who cannot say "amen" or even "bon voyage" to that?

On Wednesday, I buried a lady well into her nineties, whose husband I had buried during his eighties. Her last fourteen years were compromised. And her last three years constituted a virtual "disconnect" from reality. Finally and mercifully, as disease piled onto dis-ease, it became hospice time, DNR ("do not resuscitate") time, and cessation of food and water time. Yet still she lingered. On the twelfth night, the nurse said to her only daughter, "Is there some relative or friend she's waiting for?" "No," said her daughter. "Just me." "And have you told her it's all right to go?" the nurse continued. "No, should I?" the daughter answered. "If you feel comfortable doing so, it might help," the nurse offered. So the daughter did. And the mother died. Permission given. Permission taken.

But sometimes people come to breaking points beyond which they feel they cannot go, yet we cannot bring ourselves to view their departure as a blessing. Neither can we bring ourselves to offer our blessing. We want them alive. We want them to work harder to stay alive longer. They want to leave life's party. We want to say, "But it's early. Nobody's ready. There's so much more of it, and it won't be the same without you in it."

At one time or another, I suppose most of us have flirted with a desire to leave the party early. Call it a desire to be anywhere other than here. Not because we are clear about the "there," like heaven or Houston. We want to go because we don't want to be here. We just want out. Most of us dismiss the thought. Or repress the thought. But a few of us entertain the thought, even nurse and massage it. Yet we seldom admit the thought, because other people can't handle it, and are frankly frightened by the thought.

When we were disciplined as children—especially if we thought we were disciplined unfairly or severely— we pictured ourselves dead and everybody else sad. We also pictured them as being more than a little sorry. Mark Twain had Tom Sawyer attend his own funeral so he could listen to the eulogies of people who thought he had died. Fantasy? Of course it was fantasy. But Mark Twain wrote it knowing that children would read it and see themselves in it. But few children are serious about suicide. And most move quickly past the idea of not being here. But as people get older, some linger around the idea of not being here, and a few even act on it.

I viewed the movie *The Hours* in a nearly empty downtown Birmingham theater, and a few nights later, I reviewed it at our "Jesus @ the Oscars" seminar. The movie was considered for an Oscar for Best Picture. It is a brilliant film to analyze, but not an easy film to watch. For it engages you at levels of your life or layers of your memory that will take you deeper than you probably want to go.

As plots go, there isn't one, at least not one central one. Instead, there are three separate stories that cover a span of eighty years. Threading the stories together is a book (*Mrs. Dalloway*) and the woman who wrote it (Virginia Woolf), another woman who read it, and a third woman who more or less personified it. There is another thread, though, of self-chosen death. We're talking suicide, friends. Three considered. Two completed. My fingers were still sticky with popcorn when Nicole Kidman walked to the river, weighted her apron with a boulder, and entered the water. After she drowned, I couldn't eat another bite of my popcorn.

She left a note, though. It was meant for her husband, Leonard. She told him about the world closing in, the madness coming back, the light going out, and how it was all too much. So much, too much. Whereupon she thanked Leonard for his love, said he'd probably be able to work better with her gone, and then added, "I can't go on spoiling your life any longer."

It will probably not surprise you, given the length of my ministry, that people occasionally close the door to my office and talk to me about ending their lives. And one of the things that always surfaces is their belief that, in choosing death, they will be doing the world a favor . . . their family a favor . . . their friends a favor. Sometimes they will be quite specific about the ways in which their departure will make someone else's life easier. Those remaining will now have more time, more money, less worry, or less fury. They really believe that. Because if they didn't, they couldn't end their lives. Or wouldn't.

They are wrong, of course. Unfortunately, they are dead wrong. Once they go, nobody's life is ever better. Everybody's life is always worse. But would it make any difference if they knew that? Well, let Pat Conroy comment.

Pat Conroy is a wonderful novelist (*Lords of Discipline*, *The Great Santini*, *The Prince of Tides*, *Beach Music*). But before becoming a great novelist, Pat Conroy was a mediocre basketball player, who tells the story of his senior season at the Citadel in a brilliant book entitled *My Losing Season*.

He begins by recalling a flashy point guard, Dickie Jones, who captained the best basketball team in Citadel's history. Subsequently, Dickie went on to become the mayor of Mount Pleasant, South Carolina, and a regular communicant in the Roman Catholic Church. Yet one day, seated on a park bench in the middle of the town he governed, Dickie Jones ended his life. Pat Conroy writes:

> I had entered into another of the great drifts that my life seems to take at least once a decade. My depressions have taken on a quality of serene artistry. I find myself exploring caverns of my psyche where the stalactites are arsenic-tipped, the bats rabid, and blind pale creatures live in the lightless pools dreaming of fireflies and lanterns shivering with despair. I have a history of cracking up at least once during the writing of each of my last five books. It has not provided the greatest incentive to head for the writing table each morning, but it's the reality I've lived with. I came out of my free-fall when

I heard shrieking in Dickie's devastated home. It was Dickie's children, far too stricken to speak to me. I know the dark things that all suicides know, but as terrifying as these things were, none had prepared me for the image of my children and my family approaching my open coffin with bitterness and love tearing through them in alternating currents. My imagination has always kept me alive and it did so as I mourned for Dickie Jones's family. Out of nowhere, he had given me a sign that I was still needed in the game. The weeping and scream-ing of Dickie's devastated children saved my life. Dickie Jones died without ever knowing the great impact he had on me.[3]

At the Oscars seminar, in my review of *The Hours*, I tried to address every question posed by the movie except for one: "What do I say to someone who closes my office door and speaks of their desire to leave the party early?"

At first, I don't say much. I listen. I ask questions. I try to clarify. And I try to connect. When appropriate, I tell a little of my story, which includes the suicide of

---

3. Pat Conroy, *My Losing Season* (New York: Nan A. Talese Publisher, Doubleday, 2002), 13.

my son, Bill, because it is most likely my story that brought them in to tell their story.

I do not tell them I know what "wanting to leave" feels like. But I do tell them I know what it feels like to be left. That my life hasn't been better since Bill left. That it's been worse. For a long time . . . worse. Years of worse.

Then I say, "Look, I can't promise that things are going to turn around for you, turn up for you, or get better for you. I think they are. But if you can't see that, I can't force you to wear my glasses."

All I can say to you is this: "When you reach the point where you can't come up with a single reason to stay alive one more day, then stay alive as a gift to somebody. Maybe you'll tell them. Probably you won't. But if you stay alive as a gift for one day, you may just be able to stay alive as a gift for two days. Then who knows, maybe you can go for three."

In one of *The Hours'* other stories, Richard, who has AIDS, tells Clarissa why he doesn't want to show up to claim a literary prize he has been awarded, let alone attend the party she has planned in his honor afterwards.

Clarissa [he says], I think I'm only staying alive to satisfy you.

So [she answers], that's what you do, isn't it?

That's what people do. They stay alive for each other.

We are fast approaching the time of year when our praying and preaching will be chock full of the cross of Jesus Christ. Concerning crosses, Jesus was reported to have said, "I must bear mine, and all who would come after me must bear theirs." Notice, he did not say that all who would come after him must bear his. No, they must bear their own.

In the economy of the gospel, some (including soldiers) may be called to die for others. Others (including suicides) may be called to live for others.

Both take great courage.

March 23, 2003

epilogue

There is one remaining story I have never shared in public until now. That's because it is not my story, but Kris's. She has been marvelous through all of this. It is her desire that I publish this book, and that this story, at last, be told. Preaching these sermons has been one thing. Listening to them, when you are the preacher's wife and the subject's mother, is quite another. On the five Sundays when I have spoken openly about Bill's death, hers—listening to them—has been the harder lot.

But I promised you a story. Here it is. On the morning of the day we were to find out about Bill's death, Kris woke from a sound sleep before seven. For a number of weeks, both of us had slept fitfully, worried as we were about our son. He would have a good day, and we'd relax, which would be followed by a bad day, and we'd begin fretting again.

Upon awakening on Tuesday, May 2, Kris said she had just had the most wonderful dream. In it, Bill was happy, bubbly, confident, and vibrant—looking like his old self again—laughing, joking, doing all of his funny impressions. In the dream, he said to her, "I know you have been worried about me. But you don't have to worry anymore. Everything is all right now. Things are great now. I'm going to be fine now. Mom, it's okay." Little did Kris know that at the time she dreamed that dream, Bill had been dead for several hours.

How do we explain that? We can't. How do we understand that? We don't. How do we treat that? As a gift—for which we are grateful.